CFA Institute

AF877861

PAYMENT FOR ORDER FLOW IN THE UNITED KINGDOM

Internalisation, Retail Trading, Trade-Through Protection, and Implications for Market Structure

CFA Institute is the global association of investment professionals that sets the standards for professional excellence. We are a champion for ethical behavior in investment markets and a respected source of knowledge in the global financial community.

Our mission is to lead the investment profession globally by promoting the highest standards of ethics, education, and professional excellence for the ultimate benefit of society.

ISBN: 978-1-942713-27-2
June 2016

Contents

Executive Summary

In this paper, we investigate the clarification issued in 2012 by the Financial Services Authority (FSA), now the Financial Conduct Authority (FCA), in regard to the illegality of payment for order flow (PFOF) arrangements in the United Kingdom. A PFOF arrangement is one in which a broker offers to systematically route its order flow to a wholesale market maker in return for a fee. While the broker earns the fee (subsidising the commission charged to the end investor), the market maker acquires the opportunity to execute the order flow internally.

PFOF arrangements create a conflict of interest between the clients of the broker and the broking firm itself because the incentive to achieve best execution for each trade for each client may conflict with the incentive to maximise fees from selling order flow to market makers. In other words, PFOF arrangements may create a conflict of interest with a broker's best execution obligations. It is for this reason that the FSA decided to emphasise the ban on PFOF arrangements in 2012. Agency conflicts and client best execution are important and relevant issues in the context of investor protection and market integrity. It is helpful to understand the UK market before and after the PFOF rule clarification and the effect PFOF arrangements have had on execution quality for investors. The findings may have implications for other markets that currently permit PFOF arrangements, as well as for market structure policy more generally.

We analyse the proportion of retail-sized orders executing at the best quoted price on the UK primary market—the London Stock Exchange (LSE)—before and after the FSA's updated guidance in May 2012. We posit that the explicit removal of a potential source of revenue for brokers (and with it, a removal of potential agency conflicts) should lead to more efficient order-handling practices and a more competitive market for retail-sized orders. In addition to the prohibition of PFOF arrangements, the coincident growth of lower-cost internet execution-only accounts and the limited profitability for brokers of servicing retail clients may cause the UK retail equity market to become a more competitive, utility-like service. We observe an increase in the proportion of retail-sized trades executing at best quoted prices between 2010 and 2014 from 65% to more than 90%, which is consistent with our hypothesis.

We believe this change is a positive one for market integrity because it implies that displayed liquidity providers are rewarded with executions at the price they quote. This reward mechanism upholds market integrity by supporting the incentive to post the displayed limit orders on which price discovery is based and should lead to more aggressive quoting and competitive pricing. By contrast, this outcome may be jeopardised in markets with PFOF arrangements where internalisers are able to step ahead of the quoted price on the order book by offering price improvement. It appears that the current best execution regime in the United Kingdom appears to be working well, despite the lack of a US-style trade-through rule that explicitly prevents executions away from the best quoted price.

1. Introduction

Payment for order flow (PFOF) is the practice of market makers paying brokers (typically retail brokers) to route their clients' order flow to them in exchange for payments. PFOF enables internalisation of retail order flow by market makers. Internalisation includes broker/dealers internally executing client order flow as principal, using their own risk capital, on a systematic basis.

In May 2012, the Financial Services Authority (FSA), the precursor to the Financial Conduct Authority (FCA), issued updated guidance on the practice of PFOF in the United Kingdom (see FSA 2012). The guidance concluded that PFOF arrangements create a conflict of interest between the clients of the broker and the broking firm itself. The FSA posited that brokers operating on a regulated market and acting on behalf of a client are unlikely to satisfy the relevant rules on inducements and best execution—in effect, banning PFOF. Although PFOF was not widespread in the United Kingdom, the FSA was concerned that the practice was becoming more prevalent, particularly on the London International Financial Futures and Options Exchange (LIFFE). Additionally, best execution obligations were not being prioritised sufficiently.

Critics of modern market structure argue that internalisation under payment for order flow arrangements creates conflicts of interest with regard to order handling and routing. Specifically, PFOF arrangements call into question the ability of clients to receive best execution when brokers are incentivised to route orders to market makers paying for the privilege of having the first right to trade against such orders.

In 2014, as part of its thematic review into best execution, the (now renamed) FCA examined the progress in compliance with the updated 2012 PFOF guidelines (see FCA 2014). The FCA found that many firms had ceased to receive PFOF after the May 2012 updated guidance and a further group of firms ceased to do so in the lead-up to the thematic review (between November 2012 and October 2013). However, the FCA found that a small number of its 36 sample firms had not satisfactorily ceased to receive commission from market makers because they had unilaterally recast their own definition of their PFOF arrangements. The FCA rejected this interpretation of PFOF, reiterated its position that PFOF is inconsistent with best execution, and threatened enforcement action against any firms that continued to receive PFOF.

The guidance issued by the FSA in 2012 provides a unique, natural experiment for investigating whether the ban on PFOF has had a positive impact on market quality. We investigate this issue by calculating the percentage of retail-sized trades that execute at the best price on the main UK trading venue—the London Stock Exchange (LSE). We find that the proportion of trades executing at the best quoted price has increased between 2010 and 2014, which is consistent with a market for retail-sized orders that has become more competitive and undifferentiated because of the rise in internet execution-only trading accounts. Our study of the UK experience may allow lessons to be learned for other global markets, particularly in relation to whether trade-through protection is necessary. Our results suggest that best execution can be achieved without trade-through protection as long as the market for retail orders is competitive.

2. Technical Background

In this section we explain the concept behind payment for order flow (PFOF) and the implications it has for market structure—both positive and negative. We do this through the lens of the US market structure, where PFOF arrangements are most entrenched, which will help to emphasise the uniqueness of the UK retail service provider (RSP) model that is described later in the section.

2.1. Payment for Order Flow

Payment for order flow arrangements are typically used by broker/dealers to gain access to retail order flow in exchange for a fee. Because retail investors are typically less informed than professional or institutional investors, retail order flow is very desirable to wholesale market makers. Their information advantage means that they can internalise (i.e., trade against their own account) those retail orders that are on the wrong side of the market (i.e., against the direction of expected market movements in the short term and hence profitable to the market maker) and route any other orders to other market centres. This practice has also been referred to as "preferencing" or "cream skimming" (see, for example, Preece 2012). In essence, these market makers are buying an option on retail order flow.

Many wholesalers in the United States have PFOF agreements with retail brokerages, typically paying $0.0001 per share or less to the retail brokerage for the order flow. If the order is undesirable, it is routed to other wholesalers, internalisation pools, or exchanges for execution. The routing algorithm is determined by such factors as the depth of liquidity available in other pools, other payment for order flow arrangements, trading venue access fees, and so forth. This process of internalisation for marketable retail orders is summarised in **Figure 1**. Internalisation represents a significant proportion of overall trading activity in the United States (see, for example, Preece 2012) and is thought to account for almost 100% of all retail marketable order flow.

In order to internalise a retail order while meeting best execution obligations, broker/dealers typically provide some price improvement relative to the best market price (e.g., the national best bid and offer [NBBO] in the United States). Often, this price improvement is nominal and can be as little as $0.0001 per share. Further, this price improvement carries an opportunity cost to liquidity providers that must be balanced against the aforementioned savings provided to retail investors.

Figure 1. Retail Market Making in the United States

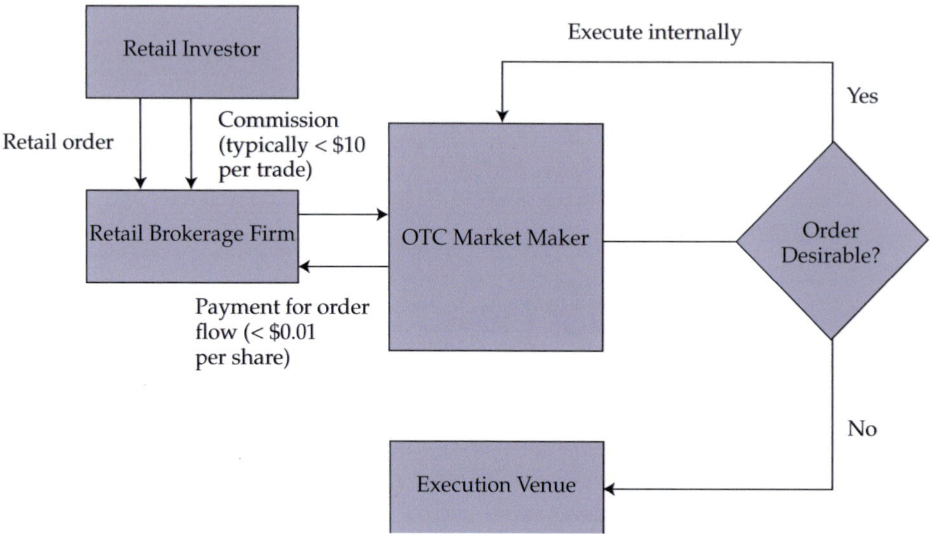

Source: Based on data from Preece (2012).

Consider, for example, a stock trading at $20.00–$20.01 at the NBBO. Internalisers fill all incoming retail marketable buy orders at $20.0099 (in front of the displayed offer) and all retail marketable sell orders at $20.0001 (in front of the displayed bid)—a nominal price improvement of $0.0001 in each case. The market makers capture the spread (minus the nominal price improvement) for themselves.

However, a retail order that gains $0.0001 in price improvement for 99 out of 100 trades observes a $0.99 total gain from price improvement (i.e., $0.0001 per share and thus $0.01 per trade of a standard 100 lot size). But if the 100th trade is a limit order for the same 100 shares that does not get executed because internalisers are stepping in front of the trade, the trader would lose $1 because of the $0.01 spread on 100 shares it would have to pay in order to trade—wiping out the price improvement from the previous 99 trades.

This example shows that price improvement may not have a net benefit for the overall market when the opportunity cost of mixed executions on limit orders is taken into account. For this reason, some jurisdictions, such as Canada and Australia, have implemented trade-at rules, which require an economically significant price improvement to justify taking trades off-exchange. However, academic research has shown that such rules may not be a panacea. For example, Foley and Putni š (2014) find evidence that minimum price improvement regulation in Canada and Australia is associated with increased spreads and does not increase the propensity of market participants to post lit liquidity (see also CFA Institute 2014).

2.2. The Market Ecosystem

Because the PFOF/internalisation paradigm does result in some price improvement, the conflicts of interest inherent in PFOF arrangements do not (and should not) typically manifest in execution prices that are "worse" than retail investors could get elsewhere. Instead, conflicts of interest arise from the nontransparent way in which these arrangements are made and the question of whether brokers pass on the full value received for selling their clients' order flow.

Further, PFOF arrangements have a significant impact on the makeup of the trading ecosystem, as shown in **Figure 2**. Consider market makers that traditionally post visible limit orders on lit venues. In today's markets, their orders would not typically interact with retail order flow (which is mostly executed off-market). Thus, market makers and institutions trading on lit venues are interacting with relatively more informed order flow (because the uninformed order flow has been filtered out by internalisers), which increases their risk of being on the wrong side of a trade. This dynamic makes the lit markets more "toxic"—or, more formally, increases the risk of adverse selection.

This increased adverse selection risk could disincentivise liquidity providers from competing at the top of the order book, which may have negative repercussions for price discovery and overall market integrity. It can also drive order flow to seek "safer" venues for execution, which helps to explain the success of dark pools that are not pre-trade transparent. In this way, order flow can self-select and self-segregate onto different types of venues—internalisers for retail flow and dark pools for institutional flow—which leaves lit venues somewhat in the lurch. To entice displayed liquidity back onto lit venues, maker-taker rebates have been introduced that provide a rebate for posted liquidity and charge a fee for taking liquidity. Maker-taker rebates create another conflict of interest for brokers because they may be incentivised to direct client trades in a manner designed to maximise the net rebate, which may not be consistent with their clients' best execution interests.

The increasing fragmentation of equity markets (along dimensions of trading venues, pretrade transparency, and trading fee structures) that has developed as venues try to cater for different types of order flow that is seeking to segment away from unattractive

Figure 2. Impact of PFOF on Market Ecosystem

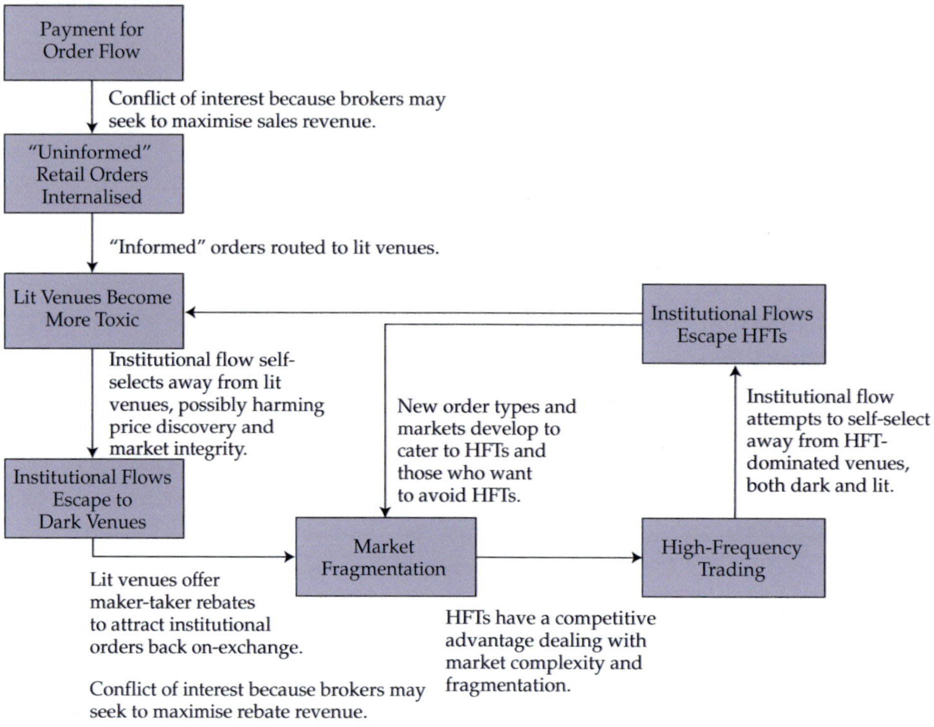

counterparties has also been blamed for the rapid rise of high-frequency traders (HFTs), who have a competitive advantage in dealing with this kind of complexity and fragmentation. Some of the strategies pursued by HFTs, such as latency arbitrage, have caused great concern and may have contributed to further self-segregation of order flow (to hide from HFTs) and market fragmentation (as venues seek to create HFT-free zones). It has been revealed that some of the venues advertising themselves as HFT-free—mostly dark pools—are misleading investors and actually hosting significant HFT volume, further eroding confidence in the market ecosystem.

2.3. Arguments in Favour of PFOF

The main argument in favour of PFOF is that it allows retail investors to benefit from the value of their order flow. The payments that retail brokers receive from market makers under PFOF arrangements indirectly benefit retail investors because these payments can subsidise the commissions that brokers charge to their customers. In comparison, on a lit exchange, retail investors would likely have to cross the spread to trade and the value of their order flow would be distributed among the market.

Perhaps with less "toxic" trading venues this spread that retail traders would be forced to cross would be lower, but it is unlikely that the retail investor would benefit. Further, simply banning PFOF arrangements will not change the fact that retail order flow is attractive and valuable due to its (on average) less-informed nature. Institutional investors will still try to seek it out, which may result in even less transparent and sub-optimal incentive arrangements as retail brokers seek to extract value from this order flow.

There is a strong case that modern markets provide retail investors with unprecedentedly low trading costs, particularly with the rise of internet execution-only accounts. Whether this change is a net positive for the market ecosystem is a different question. There is an argument that the traditional distinction between a retail and an institutional investor is no longer relevant because most average "investors" are invested in the stock market via investment and pension schemes and other retirement accounts. They are thus also institutional investors and may lose out from increased adverse selection on markets because their fund manager has to incur the associated trading costs (in the form of potentially higher spreads, market impact, opportunity costs, and so on). However, the US Securities and Exchange Commission (SEC), for example, has explicitly made the point that it seeks to protect individual retail investors, implying that this argument is not a compelling one.

Users of internet execution-only accounts today are likely predominantly day traders or, in academic parlance, "noise traders." Their order flow is also typically considered to be, on average, uninformed and is thus valuable for professional traders and market makers. However, critics argue that allowing PFOF arrangements in order to provide price improvement to noise traders at the expense of a complex and fragmented market ecosystem (and possibly a worse ecosystem for the average investor's mutual fund and pension fund investments) is not a good trade off.

2.4. Retail Trading in the United Kingdom: The Retail Service Provider Model

The discussion in Sections 2.1–2.3 presents the issues with and advantages and disadvantages of a market where PFOF arrangements are commonplace. In 2012, the FSA took the view that this balance of advantages and disadvantages was not in the interests of clients and issued a clarification prohibiting the use of PFOF arrangements in the United Kingdom. Before analysing the impact of this clarification in Section 3, it is informative to examine the way in which retail investors can trade equities in the United Kingdom, which is different from the US experience.

First, to reiterate, there are no PFOF arrangements. There is also less retail trading (a stylised fact across Europe), with individual day traders (for example) more likely to use spread betting and contract for difference (CFD) platforms because of the requirement to pay stamp duty (i.e., a tax) on equities in the United Kingdom. Further, the cost of data and post-trade settlement in the UK is large relative to that in the US. Retail trades, which are not netted, would thus have to pay potentially high clearing fees.

Second, retail trading is based on the retail service provider (RSP) model, shown in **Figure 3**, which is essentially an internal market of market makers that each broker cultivates for processing retail orders. It is possible to think of RSPs providing some of the benefits of a virtual consolidated NBBO for retail brokers (APCIMS 2011), which helps to deliver competitive pricing to the end investors in a market with no consolidated tape (as is the case in the United Kingdom).

A retail order placed with a broker is announced to the RSP network of market makers. Market makers bid for the retail orders, and the best price will be selected for the client as per best execution requirements. Firm prices and sizes must be quoted, and investors have complete execution certainty. Investors typically have a short time frame (about 30 seconds) to confirm or reject the quoted terms of trade. Neither the broker nor the market maker pay any per-trade costs (e.g., fees or commissions) other than a subscription fee to the network software provider, which operates the RSP system (e.g., Proquote or Fidessa).

Trades are completed on an agency basis so that client assets are not pooled with the assets of the counterparties, which is also facilitated by the single-execution and single-settlement characteristics (i.e., straight-through processing) of the RSP model (see APCIMS 2013). The trades are typically reported to the London Stock Exchange, although any recognised investment exchange (RIE) is suitable. In the past, the PLUS Stock Exchange gained significant RSP reporting market share because it offered free trade reporting. RSP trades are recorded as on-exchange trades despite being consummated off-book (as per the Markets in Financial Instruments Directive, or MiFID), and thus, retail investors benefit from the full protection of exchange rules in the case of default (APCIMS 2013). The RSP model developed as a response to broker demand for ways to obtain and evidence best execution for their clients, a requirement that was established in the United Kingdom before MiFID mandated it in the European Union.

Figure 3. Retail Market Making in the United Kingdom

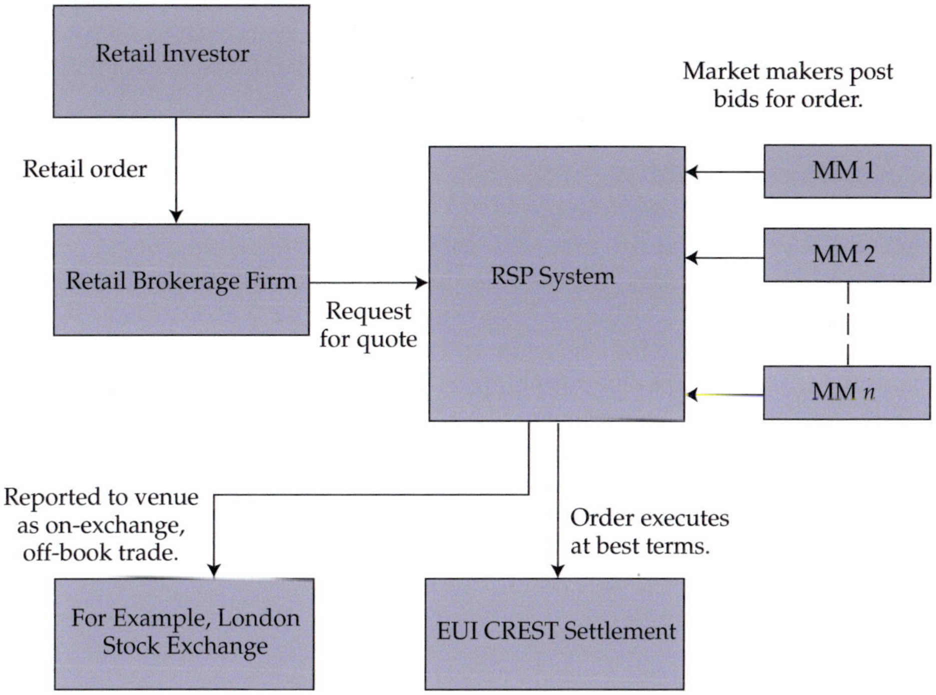

Source: Based on data from APCIMS (2013).

Data from Compeer, a provider of operational data on the UK wealth management industry, suggest that in 2014, there were approximately 23.5 million retail trades undertaken on behalf of individuals (Compeer 2015). Ninety-five percent of these trades were through the RSP system described in Figure 3. Of these private client trades, 17.1 million (73%) were execution-only trades, whereas 6.4 million (27%) were completed via full-service wealth managers. There were approximately 11.5 million and 4.5 million execution-only and full-service cash market equity trades, respectively, in 2014. The balance of trades was for CFD/spread bets and collectives (funds). Interestingly, Compeer notes that the main growth in trading occurs in execution-only collectives, which is intuitive given the rise of internet execution-only services. Such services naturally suit self-directed investors who would also likely prefer the relatively lower risk profile, and lower explicit trading costs, of collective investment schemes.

Compeer further notes that in 2014, the average commission per trade was £12, significantly lower than the average cost per trade of £18.75—an issue for execution-only brokers because it suggests that efficiency gains have not resulted in the hoped-for fall in costs per trade. Meanwhile, however, competition has been putting downward pressure on commission income, which is good news for investors: Compeer is predicting single-digit commissions per trade.

In 2010, IFS LiquidMetrix (2010) analysed retail off-exchange trading in the United Kingdom using a one-week sample of PLUS exchange trades—a popular venue for the reporting RSP trades at the time. IFS looked at price improvement offered and found that most UK retail trades received price improvement on the order of 14 bps (or about 20% of the spread). According to IFS, using touch price (i.e., assuming that the entire trade can be filled at the best bid/offer without considering available depth at the top of the book) as the basis for determining price improvement, rather than a depth-weighted trading cost, is misleading because it artificially improves the benchmark price, even though that price may not be achievable in the real world. It concludes that the RSP model provides value to retail investors above and beyond a hypothetical consolidated "best European on-book" price.

3. Data Analysis

The purpose of this study is to examine the execution quality of retail-sized orders on the UK primary market—the London Stock Exchange—before and after the FSA's updated guidance banning PFOF arrangements in May 2012. It is our understanding that prior to the updated guidance being issued, the FSA engaged in industry outreach on the subject of PFOF and, as a result, it is possible that changes in behaviour by brokers and market makers may have occurred before the guidance was issued in May 2012. For this reason, a formal event study with May 2012 as time zero may not be the appropriate specification.

We take a different approach and examine execution quality and market integrity by looking at the proportion of retail-sized orders that executed at the best quoted price. Given the discussion in Section 2, we posit that a market ecosystem that does not have PFOF (and its associated incentive structure) will have less scope for capturing retail order flow by offering price improvement and internalising retail-sized orders.

At the same time, without trade-through protection of the displayed quote in the United Kingdom, retail-sized orders rely on competition between market makers and best execution obligations to achieve good outcomes. Given the limited profitability of executing retail order flow and the continuing growth of internet execution-only accounts, it seems likely that executing retail flow may become a competitive, utility-like service, where orders are simply executed at the best quoted price. The purpose of calculating price improvement statistics is to examine whether the UK market has become any more or less competitive for retail-sized orders following the updated PFOF guidance in May 2012.

3.1. Sample

Data for the UK market are from IFS LiquidMetrix in raw exchange message form. Data on quotes and trades were collected for the periods described in **Table 1**. The sample period shown in Table 1 (broadly, 2010–2014) is based on Rosov (2015), which, in turn, is based on the ideas in Alampieski and Lepone (2011). A comprehensive set of statistics on the base data set can be found in Rosov (2015). For each calendar month, two days of data were collected. Data availability largely dictated the sample selection (and the exceptions listed). For each day, data were collected from the LSE on 50 stocks split evenly into 25 large-cap and 25 small-cap groups (the list of sample stocks is available upon request).

Table 1. Sample Period Selection

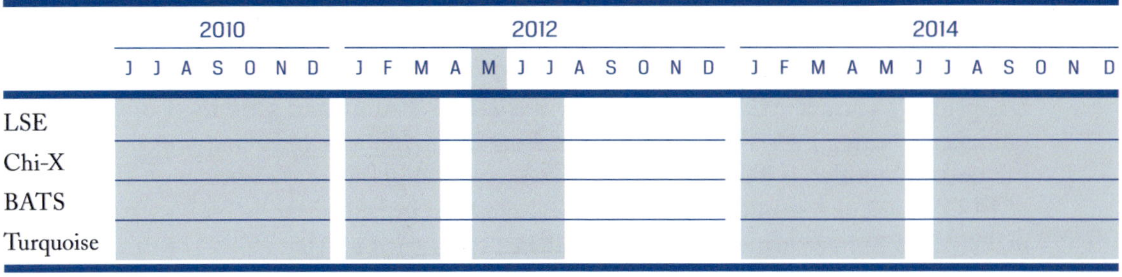

Note: The shaded blue indicates the months for which data are available. The updated PFOF guidance was released in May 2012.

For the purposes of the RSP model, other UK stock exchanges for which we have data, Chi-X and Turquoise, are not immediately relevant because they are not classified as RIEs and, therefore, RSP trades cannot be reported to them. Prior to 2012, the RSPs used the London Stock Exchange and PLUS Stock Exchange to report trades. However, in May 2012 (coincidentally, the same time as the FSA clarification), it was announced that the PLUS Stock Exchange would cease operations, leaving only the LSE as an RIE. Subsequently, PLUS was purchased by ICAP and continued operations after being renamed ISDX. In May 2013, it was announced that BATS Europe would become an RIE, although, to the best of our knowledge, the vast majority of RSP trades continue to be reported to either the LSE or the ISDX. For these reasons, we limit our data sample to the London Stock Exchange. The guidance on PFOF in the United Kingdom was issued in May 2012, so our sample will enable us to compare the market quality before and after this change.

We reconstruct the order book to a depth of five levels. We then follow the method used in IFS (2010) and take each trade that has a value below £7,000 and compare the trade price with the best available price in the market as if a market order of equal size were sent to the market at that instant. We use £7,000 because it is the approximate size of the average RSP trade in FTSE100 stocks and is close to the MiFID definition of a retail-size trade (7,500). Two benchmark prices for calculating price improvement are used:

1. Using the "touch" price as the effective trade price (i.e., executing the entire trade at the top of the book, effectively ignoring depth) or

2. Using the "depth-weighted" price (i.e., filling the observed order size through the book and taking the weighted average price as the best available price).

These two prices are compared with the actual trade price to determine the level, if any, of price improvement. For example, let's assume the order book looks as shown in **Table 2**.

Consider a sale trade that was executed at 20.005 for 400 shares. The true revenue from this trade to the client was 8,002 (20.005 × 400). Were the client to sell 400 shares at the best bid price of 20.00 (i.e., the touch), the revenue would have been 8,000, and so the price improvement relative to the touch is 0.005 [(8,002 – 8,000)/400] per share. However, this benchmark is clearly artificially high because there are not 400 shares at the top of the book. The depth-weighted revenue of selling shares down through the book would be 7,996 (100 × 20.00 + 200 × 19.99 + 100 × 19.98), and so, the price improvement is more accurately 0.015 [(8,002 – 7,996)/400] per share.

3.2. Results for the LSE

Table 3 displays the price improvement descriptive statistics for the London Stock Exchange. The results, which are for the entire sample and are not segregated by date, show that price improvement tends to occur for stocks with a higher spread (reflecting larger price improvement for small-cap stocks). For example, the average price improvement trade is on a stock with a spread of 14.2 bps, which compares with a spread of 8.1 bps for trades at the best bid/offer (BBO). The average level of price improvement relative to the touch price (i.e., assuming the whole trade can be executed at the top of the book) is 3.8 bps. But if we compare price improvement with the more realistic depth-weighted benchmark price, trades receive almost 5.7 bps of price improvement, capturing 27.7%

Table 2. Sample Order Book

Depth	Bid	Offer	Depth
		20.03	300
		20.02	200
		20.01	100
100	20.00		
200	19.99		
300	19.98		

of the spread on average (midpoint trades capture 50% of the spread by definition). The interpretation of the spread capture statistic is that if the top of the order book is 20.00–20.10, the trade price would be 20.027 for a sale or 20.073 for a buy.

Table 3 shows that on the primary exchange in the United Kingdom, the LSE, 82.5% of trades are executed at the BBO, which is to be expected given the best execution obligations. More accurately, this statistic tells us that in 82.5% of cases, the true cost of the trade (i.e., trade size × trade price) is the same as the depth-weighted cost (i.e., trade size × best price on order book). Only 3.6% of trades are executed at a worse price, which likely reflects the challenge of recreating a completely accurate BBO (given the limitations of the dataset and the lack of both trade-through protection and a consolidated tape). Most interestingly, 13.9% of trades on the LSE are executed with price improvement (9.5% with some price improvement and 4.4% at the midpoint).

Table 4 and **Figure 4** present descriptive statistics for the LSE segregated by market cap and year. The statistics suggest that average spreads for large-cap stocks have not experienced a significant and/or secular change, rising slightly between 2010 and 2012 and falling subsequently by 2014. The previously observed pattern of price improvement occurring on average for stocks with higher spreads remains across all years and market-cap buckets. The proportion of the spread captured by the price improvement is approximately 20%–25% for small-cap stocks and 25%–30% for large caps—reflecting the smaller spread (denominator) on large caps.

Table 3. Descriptive Statistics for UK Data

Relative to Quoted Best Price	Value Traded (£ millions)	Number of Trades	Average Quoted Spread (bps)	Average Touch Price Improvement (bps)	Average Spread Capture (%)	Average Depth Price Improvement (bps)	% of Trades
Worse	3,088	123,324	8.8	–4.5	–70.8	–6.4	3.6
Same	2,763	2,854,533	8.1	0.0	0.0	0.0	82.5
Better	2,877	328,933	14.2	3.8	27.7	5.7	9.5
Midpoint	2,781	152,463	11.5	5.8	50.0	6.0	4.4

Notes: Average Touch Price Improvement compares the true cost of the trade with the cost of the trade were the entire size of the trade executed at the best quoted price. Average Depth Price Improvement compares the true cost of the trade with the cost of the trade were the trade executed at the weighted average price given the depth of the order book at each price level.

Table 4. Descriptive Statistics for LSE

Relative to Quoted Best Price	Value Traded (£ millions)	Number of Trades	Average Quoted Spread (bps)	Average Touch Price Improvement (bps)	Average Spread Capture (%)	Average Depth Price Improvement (bps)	% of Trades
Large cap							
2010							
Worse	3,461	27,748	7.1	–4.6	–81.9	–7	3.3
Same	2,843	570,175	6.8	0.0	0	0	67.3
Better	3,112	172,780	9.9	2.8	27.4	4	20.4
Midpoint	2,869	76,359	11.3	5.6	50	5.9	9
2012							
Worse	3,076	29,153	7.8	–4.1	–68.4	–5	3.5
Same	2,620	687,565	7.1	0	0	0	82.9
Better	2,823	73,527	10.3	3.1	29.3	4.1	8.9
Midpoint	2,689	38,986	10.8	5.4	50	5.5	4.7
2014							
Worse	3,169	55,164	4.7	–3.2	–67.6	–3.4	3.7
Same	3,005	1,375,105	4.6	0.0	0.0	0.0	91.9
Better	3,093	37,161	6.7	2.6	32.2	3.6	2.5
Midpoint	2,915	27,881	6.6	4.2	50.0	4.4	1.9
Small cap							
2010							
Worse	2,276	3,970	29.9	–12.5	–75.6	–33.7	3.7
Same	1,950	70,896	21.3	0	0	0	65.6
Better	2,166	27,272	42.9	9.5	21	17.2	25.3
Midpoint	2,400	5,811	23.5	11.8	50	13.4	5.4
2012							
Worse	1,448	4,574	24.5	–8.9	57.5	–18	4.5
Same	1,355	77,831	27.2	0	0	0	76.8
Better	1,506	16,017	40.5	9.7	24.9	15.8	15.8
Midpoint	1,462	2,961	27.6	13.8	50	15.9	2.9

(continued)

Table 4. Descriptive Statistics for LSE (continued)

Relative to Quoted Best Price	Value Traded (£ millions)	Number of Trades	Average Quoted Spread (bps)	Average Touch Price Improvement (bps)	Average Spread Capture (%)	Average Depth Price Improvement (bps)	% of Trades
2014							
Worse	1,387	2,265	28.4	−20.3	−60.9	−19.1	2.9
Same	1,236	72,961	28.8	0.0	0.0	0.0	93.8
Better	1,269	2,076	35.0	12.1	27.3	15.9	2.7
Midpoint	1,082	465	35.8	26.4	50.0	31.3	0.6

Notes: Average Touch Price Improvement compares the true cost of the trade with the cost of the trade were the entire size of the trade executed at the best quoted price. Average Depth Price Improvement compares the true cost of the trade with the cost of the trade were the trade executed at the weighted average price given the depth of the order book at each price level.

The descriptive statistics in Table 4 show that in 2010, approximately 67.3% of trades in large-cap stocks were executed at the best price (65.6% for small caps). Large (small) caps were executed with some price improvement 29.4% (30.7%) of the time, of which 9% (5.4%) were at the midpoint. In 2012, we observe a significant jump in the proportion of small caps executing at the best price (up to 76.8% from 65.6% in 2010) and an even greater increase for large caps (up to 82.9% from 67.3% in 2010). It seems in both cases, the proportion of midpoint trades approximately halved, as did the proportion of trades receiving some price improvement. The proportion of trades executing at worse than the depth-weighted BBO is stable at around 3.0%–3.5% for large caps and around 4.5%–5.5% for small caps. By 2014, the statistics show that these trends have continued, with 93.8% of small-cap trades occurring at the best price (an increase from 2012) while 91.9% of large-cap trades do so.

In summary, we observe an increase in the proportion of retail-sized trades occurring at the best price on the London Stock Exchange between 2010 and 2014. These findings are consistent with improved integrity of the best quoted price (i.e., the price quoted is the one that can be traded at).

This finding is interesting in the light of the 2012 clarification by the FSA in regards to PFOF. The motivation for this clarification was concern on the FSA's part as to the quality of adherence to best execution standards and evidence of some payment for order flow arrangements on the London International Financial Futures and Options Exchange (LIFFE) market.

Figure 4. Execution at Best Quoted Prices on the LSE

A. Large-Cap Stocks

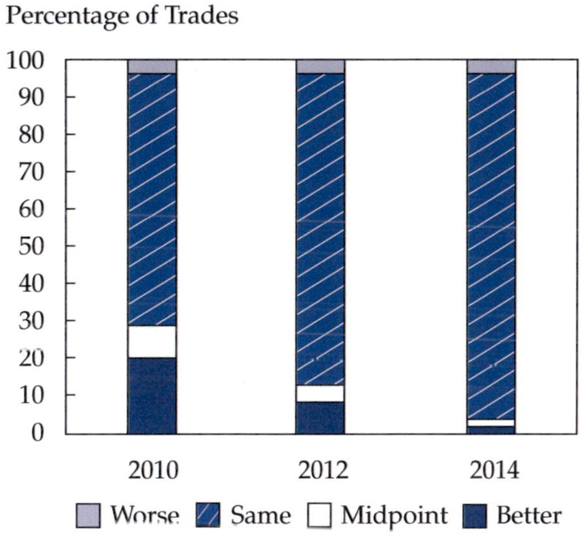

B. Small-Cap Stocks

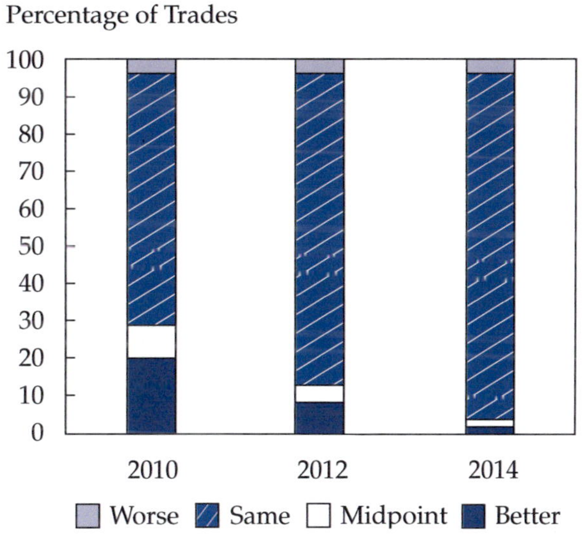

Note: These diagrams show the proportion of trades executing at different prices relative to the best quoted price on the LSE.

3.3. Retail Trading in France

We also compare the United Kingdom with another market where PFOF does not play a significant role—France. The UK and French markets are qualitatively similar in the sense that they are both operating under MiFID best execution provisions, which makes the comparison valid and may provide some comfort as to the reliability of the UK results.

The tradition for retail equity trading in France is not as well established as in the United States or even the United Kingdom. The comprehensive pension system means investing for retirement has not been widespread. A concentration rule (prior to MiFID) meant that all retail orders were routed to the exchange and were not intermediated by market makers. Most of this kind of trading occurred through retail banks that offered trading services as part of their suite of product offerings. As a result, post-MiFID, the French retail banks had large user networks but trading by retail accounts was, on average, very low (on the order of one order per account per year).

Today, occasional retail traders will continue to execute via the services provided by their retail banks, and most of this flow is routed to the primary exchange, Euronext. However, some retail banks offer a suite of account options, some of which allow users to opt in or opt out of having their orders routed to alternative venues, including Systematic Internalisers, Multilateral Trading Facilities, or crossing networks. Finally, a financial transaction tax (FTT) was introduced at a rate of 0.2 bps per share on blue-chip stock trades (defined as the shares of companies with a market cap greater than 1 billion). In a manner similar to the UK experience with stamp duty, the FTT is paid at the settlement level, making CFD platforms more attractive for casual traders. In this market ecosystem, PFOF arrangements have never been used or proposed to any material extent by market participants.

The statistics for 2014 for French stocks listed on Euronext are qualitatively similar to those for the United States (and are available upon request), with around 92% of large-cap and 86% of small-cap stocks executing at the best quoted price. Rates of price improvement and midpoint execution are below 2% and 1%, respectively. These figures are qualitatively similar to the UK market results in Section 3.2 and are consistent with a MiFID best execution regime that is yielding similar results despite differences in member states' domestic retail equity markets. Overall, these findings lend validity to the results for the UK market.

4. Conclusions and Implications

In May 2012, the FSA issued a clarification emphasising that existing rules on best execution and inducements did not permit payment for order flow arrangements. Implicit in this statement is that PFOF was possible in the United Kingdom, and we believe this clarification was motivated by concerns that best execution was not being sufficiently strictly adhered to as well as by some evidence of PFOF arrangements in other UK markets.

We examine the proportion of retail-sized orders that execute at the quoted best price on the United Kingdom's main trading venue—the London Stock Exchange—and find that this proportion has increased between 2010 and 2014. These findings are consistent with our hypothesis and the following narrative about the UK retail equity market:

1. The loss of a potential source of revenue from retail PFOF arrangements across asset classes, combined with the low profitability of servicing retail clients—particularly given the continued popularity of internet execution-only services—has caused retail-sized equity order execution to become a competitive, utility like service.

2. The implication of the first point is that the current best execution regime appears to be working well, despite the lack of a US-style trade-through rule that would explicitly protect quotes at the top of the order book. There does not seem to be an obvious driver for regulatory reform in this area.

3. Further, it is possible that markets that do have trade-through protection, such as the US market, may not need this explicit quote protection to maintain best execution. This suggestion is interesting given that some market participants argue that trade-through protection increases the technical complexity of the market ecosystem, leaving it open to high-frequency strategies like latency arbitrage.

4. Finally, it is interesting to note that the move in the United Kingdom toward execution at the best price has been at the expense of trades executing with price improvement (or at the midpoint). We argue that this is a positive change for market integrity overall because it implies that displayed liquidity providers are being rewarded with executions at the price they quote, something that may not be happening in markets with PFOF where internalisers are able to step ahead of the quoted price on the order book. This reward mechanism upholds market integrity because it supports the incentive to post displayed limit orders, on which price discovery is based.

References

Alampieski, K., and A. Lepone. 2011. "High Frequency Trading Firms, Order Book Participation, and Liquidity Supply during Periods of Heightened Adverse Selection Risk: Evidence from LSE, BATS and Chi-X." Working paper (www.ecmcrc.org/Articles/High_Frequency_Trading_firms,orderbook_participation_and_liquidity_supply_during_periods_of_heightened_adverse_selection_risk-Evidence_from_LSE,BATS_and_Chi-X.pdf).

APCIMS. 2011. "Response from the Association of Private Client Investment Managers and Stockbrokers." Consultation response, Association of Private Client Investment Managers and Stockbrokers (www.thewma.co.uk/uploads/files/29/apcims_response_to_mifid_review_february2011.pdf).

———. 2013. "The UK Retail Service Provider (RSP) Model: An Explanatory Note." Association of Private Client Investment Managers and Stockbrokers.

CFA Institute. 2014. "Trade-At Rules in Australia and Canada: A Mixed Bag for Investors." Policy brief (November): www.cfainstitute.org/ethics/Documents/Policy%20Brief_Trade-at%20Rules.pdf.

Compeer. 2015. "UK Wealth Management Industry Report 2015."

Foley, S., and T.J. Putniņš. 2014. "Regulatory Efforts to Reduce Dark Trading in Canada and Australia: How Have They Worked?" Research report, CFA Institute (2 October): www.cfainstitute.org/ethics/Documents/Trade-at%20Rule%20Report.pdf.

FCA. 2014. "Best Execution and Payment for Order Flow." Thematic review, Financial Conduct Authority (July).

FSA. 2012. "Guidance on the Practice of Payment for Order Flow." Finalised guidance, Financial Services Authority (May).

IFS. 2010. "Retail Off-Book Share Trading in the UK." White paper, Intelligent Financial Systems (20 May): www.if5.com/liquidmetrix/Articles/LM004.

Preece, R. 2012. "Dark Pools, Internalization, and Equity Market Quality." CFA Institute (October): www.cfapubs.org/doi/pdf/10.2469/ccb.v2012.n5.1.

Preece, R., and S. Rosov. 2014. "Dark Trading and Equity Market Quality." *Financial Analysts Journal*, vol. 70, no. 6 (November/December): 33–48.

Rosov, S. 2015. "Liquidity in Equity Markets: Characteristics, Dynamics, and Implications for Market Quality." CFA Institute (August).

CFA Institute

AUTHOR

Sviatoslav Rosov, PhD, CFA
Analyst
Capital Markets Policy

CONTRIBUTORS

Rhodri Preece, CFA
Head
Capital Markets Policy
EMEA

Kurt N. Schacht, CFA
Managing Director
Standards and Advocacy

We also wish to thank, in alphabetical order, James Brown (head of client services, Compeer), David Curran (chief operating officer, execution and trading, Peel Hunt), Dennis Dick, CFA (proprietary trader and market structure consultant, Bright Trading), and Andy Thompson (director, Wealth Management Association) for their comments. All errors are our own.

Made in the USA
Monee, IL
09 November 2026

67972907R00019